Now What?

Empowering Graduates on Their Career Journeys

By

Myriam C. Muniz

Independently published
Momentum Moves Mountains
May 2025

Dedication

To my daughter, Zahra,

Your journey through college and into your profession as a Physician Assistant has been nothing short of inspiring.

Your perseverance, determination, and unwavering spirit have shown me the power of never giving up. I am truly proud of the amazing woman you've become.

This book is for you and for every new graduate stepping into the world of adulting and career-building. May it bring encouragement, guidance, and the reassurance that with hard work and faith, success is always within reach.

With all my love and pride,
Mami

This second book would not have been possible without the support, guidance, and inspiration of so many incredible people in my life:

My Husband – Your unwavering encouragement and constant belief in my dreams have been my foundation. Thank you for always cheering me on and reminding me to keep pushing forward. You are my greatest supporter, and I couldn't do this without you.

Kristin Dishaw – From the very beginning, you've been on this journey with me, offering invaluable feedback on everything—presentations, books, and even naming the company Momentum Moves Mountains. Your belief in me and in every project I've undertaken has been a source of strength and inspiration. Thank you for your friendship, guidance, and unwavering support.

Zahra – Your editorial feedback brought both clarity and heart to this book. Watching your journey to becoming a Physician Assistant has been a source of immense pride and inspiration. I'm so grateful for your thoughtful insights and for the incredible person you are.

The Graduates and Early Career Professionals – You are the reason for this book. Your determination and courage to navigate the early stages of your careers inspire me every day. I hope the lessons and encouragement shared here will help you embrace your own journeys and find success in your chosen paths.

To everyone who has contributed to this book—whether through feedback, encouragement, or inspiration—thank you from the bottom of my heart. Your support means everything to me.

First Edition

Printed in the United States of America

ISBN: 9798281281485

Independently published

For permissions or inquiries, contact:
myriam.c.muniz@gmail.com

Table of Contents

Now What?

Empowering Graduates on Their Career Journeys

Introduction: A New Chapter Begins

Querido Diario,

Today feels like the beginning of something big. It's not just another day; it's the start of my new journey as a mentor. I can still remember the first time I met Jamie and how her guidance changed my life. Her insights and encouragement helped me navigate the rocky waters of my career change, and now it's my turn to pay it forward.

As I think about Jeremy and Kristina, I feel a mix of excitement and nervousness. They're both stepping into their new careers, and I can't help but wonder if I can offer them the same support that Jamie gave me. Jeremy, with his analytical mind, is ready to tackle the world of finance, while Kristina, a passionate mechanic, is determined to break barriers in a male-dominated field. I admire their ambition and can't wait to help them find their footing.

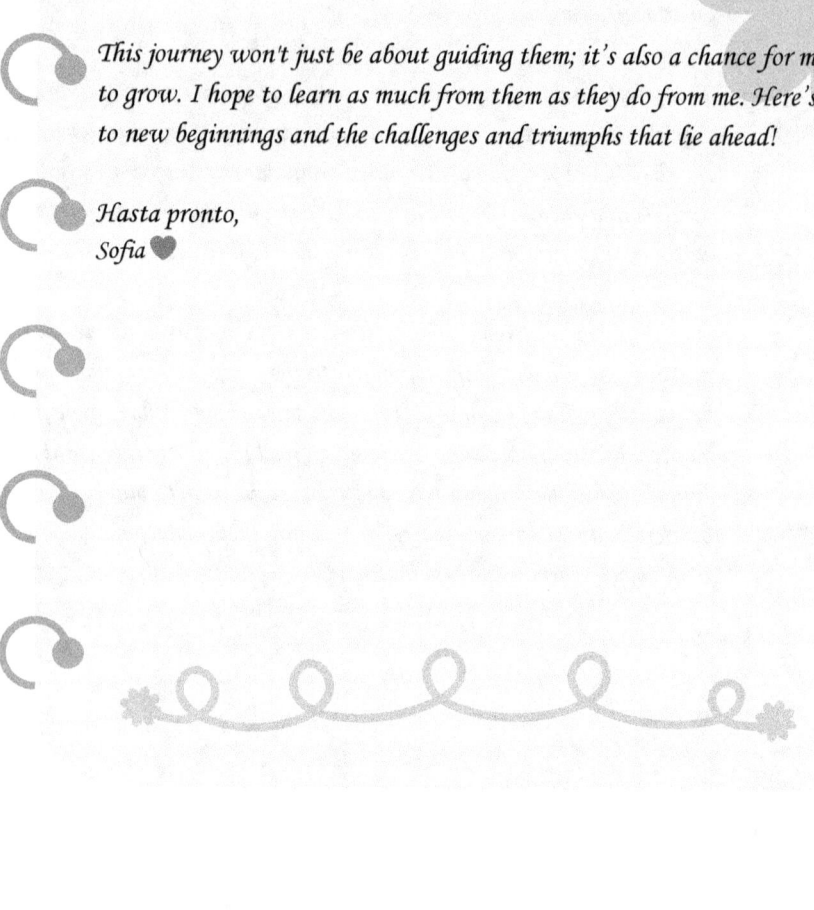

This journey won't just be about guiding them; it's also a chance for me to grow. I hope to learn as much from them as they do from me. Here's to new beginnings and the challenges and triumphs that lie ahead!

Hasta pronto,
Sofia 🖤

Sofia:

Hey Jamie! I wanted to share some exciting news! 🌟 I'm officially mentoring Jeremy and Kristina as they start their careers!

Jamie:

That's amazing, Sofia! I'm so proud of you! 🎉 How are you feeling about it?

Honestly, a little nervous. I want to make sure I'm as helpful to them as you were to me. Any tips on how to approach mentoring?

Absolutely! Just be yourself. Remember, it's about listening and sharing your experiences. Your journey can inspire them, just like mine inspired you. ⭐

That makes sense. I want to create an open space for them where they feel comfortable sharing their struggles and successes.

Definitely! Encourage them to ask questions and share their fears. That openness will foster trust and growth. You've got this, Sofia! I believe in you.

Thanks, Jamie! Your support means the world to me. I'll keep you updated on how it goes! 😊

Can't wait to hear all about it! You're going to be an incredible mentor. Let's catch up soon!

Chapter 1: Starting with Sofia's Story

Querido Diario,

I can't believe how much has changed in just a short time. A few months ago, I was stuck in a job that sucked the life out of me. It wasn't just the long hours or the never-ending meetings; it was the feeling of being trapped in a life that wasn't mine. Every morning, I would wake up and think, ¿Qué estoy haciendo? (What am I doing?). I had to make a change.

The turning point came one day when I was sitting on a park bench, feeling the weight of everything around me, and I realized I couldn't keep going like this. My soul was telling me to stop. I needed a new path. That's when I called Jamie, my career coach, and told her I wanted to leave everything behind and become a project manager. I felt nervous and unsure, but Jamie didn't let me doubt myself. She helped me understand the power of networking, the importance of building relationships, and most importantly, the value of believing in myself.

With her guidance, I took the leap. I enrolled in a project management course, and though there were times I doubted myself, I kept going. I reached out to people, I went to networking events, and little by little, I started building my confidence. Every time I connected with someone, I felt more empowered. That's when I realized something: it wasn't just the job that was going to change my life, it was the people around me.

And now, here I am. I've officially made the switch to project management, and it feels incredible. I can't believe I'm living my dream! But the journey isn't over. Now, I'm mentoring Jeremy and

Kristina as they embark on their own career paths, and I'm so excited to be part of their growth. I know that I couldn't have done it without Jamie's support, and now, I'm ready to give back, just like she did for me.

As I guide Jeremy and Kristina, I'll be leaning on Jamie again. She's always there for me, and I know she'll help me be the best mentor I can be. We're all in this together, si Dios quiere (God willing), and I can't wait to see where this journey takes us. Here's to embracing change, taking risks, and making things happen.

Hasta pronto,
Sofia ♥

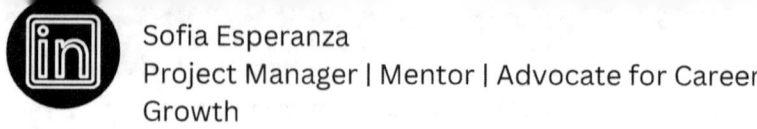

Sofia Esperanza
Project Manager | Mentor | Advocate for Career Growth

✦ Exciting News! ✦

I'm thrilled to share that today marks a new chapter in my life! After months of personal growth and a lot of soul-searching, I've transitioned from a corporate career to pursuing my true passion—project management. 🎉

This journey has been full of challenges, but each step has taught me something new. Here are a few key lessons I've learned along the way:

1. Embrace Change:
Change can be intimidating, but it's often the catalyst for discovering what you're really meant to do. Don't be afraid to step outside your comfort zone and follow what excites you. It's never too late to reinvent yourself!

2. Seek Support:
Throughout my journey, having the support of those around me has been invaluable. My mentor, Jamie, has been a guiding light, offering wisdom and encouragement when I needed it most. Surround yourself with people who believe in your potential.

3. Stay Resilient:
The road to your dream career is not without its bumps, but don't let setbacks stop you. Every challenge is a chance to grow stronger and learn. Keep pushing forward—you've got this!

4. Celebrate Your Progress:
No achievement is too small to celebrate. Take time to acknowledge each step forward. Every little win brings you closer to your goal.

And now, as I take on the role of mentoring Jeremy and Kristina, I'm excited to help them navigate their own career paths. I never imagined that along with my passion for project management, I'd also be mentoring others, but it's been an incredibly fulfilling part of my journey. Here's to new beginnings and the opportunities that lie ahead! ✨

#CareerChange #ProjectManagement #Mentorship #EmbraceChange #NewBeginnings #PursueYourPassion

Reflect on Your Journey: Take a moment to write about your own career path. What challenges have you faced? What pivotal moments have shaped your decisions? Consider keeping a journal like Sofia to track your thoughts and progress.

Embrace Change: If you feel stuck, think about what changes you'd like to make in your career. What steps can you take to pursue your passions? Write down one change you can implement this week.

Seek Support: Identify a mentor, a trusted friend or a career coach who can guide you. Reach out to them and share your goals. Don't hesitate to ask for advice or encouragement.

Set S.M.A.R.T. Goals: Break down big dreams into achievable steps. Focus on short-term, realistic goals that lead to long-term success — and celebrate each win along the way!

Join a Community: Consider joining a group or networking with others in your desired field. Engaging with like-minded individuals can provide motivation and open doors to new opportunities.

Remember, every journey starts with a single step. Embrace the process, and don't forget to enjoy the ride!

Chapter 2:
Meeting Jeremy the Financial Analyst

Sofia:

Hey Jeremy! ☀ I heard you're starting your new role as a Financial Analyst soon. How are you feeling about it?

Jeremy:

Hey Sofia! I'm excited but also super nervous! It's a big step into the corporate world, and I just hope I'm ready for it. 🧑‍💼

Totally understandable! I felt the same way when I started my career. Remember, it's okay to feel nervous—it just means you care! What are you most looking forward to?

I'm really excited to learn and get hands-on experience. I just want to make a good impression and prove that I belong there.

You definitely belong there! Just focus on learning and growing. I'd recommend reaching out to a few colleagues once you start. Networking is key in finance.

That makes sense! I'll do that. Thanks, Sofia! Any other tips for me as I start?

Absolutely! Keep a learning mindset, ask questions, and don't be afraid to seek out mentorship. You've got this! 💪

Querido Diario,

Watching Jeremy prepare for his role as a Financial Analyst brings back a wave of memories from my own early career days. His excitement is palpable, but so is the nervousness that comes with stepping into the unknown. I can see the potential in him; he has a keen analytical mind and a natural curiosity that will serve him well in finance.

I remember feeling that same mix of excitement and fear. I worried about fitting in and proving myself, just like Jeremy. Those early days taught me invaluable lessons about resilience and self-belief.

Jeremy is already off to a great start by seeking advice and actively preparing for his role. I see a lot of promise in him, and I'm excited to guide him on this journey. My hope is that he embraces every challenge, learns from his experiences, and grows into a confident professional. I can't wait to see where this path leads him!

Hasta pronto,
Sofia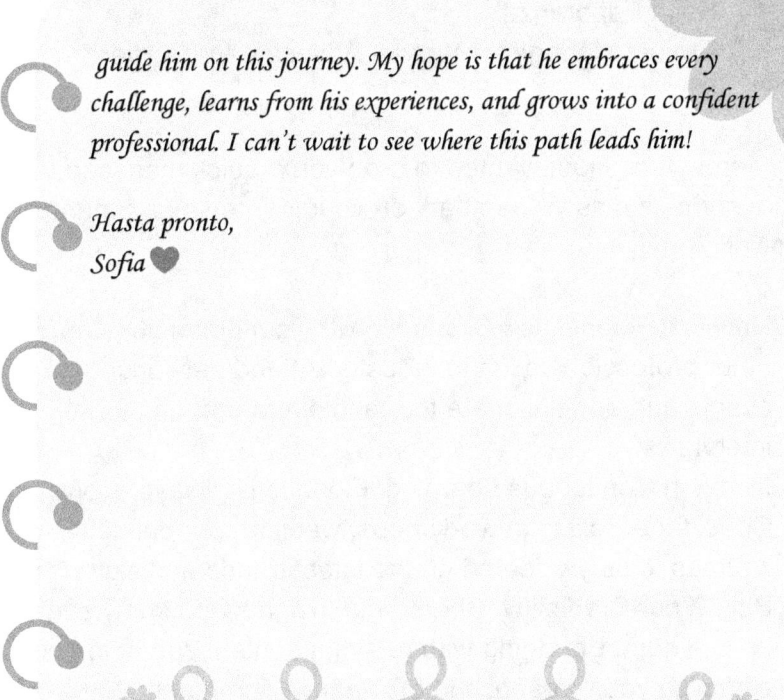

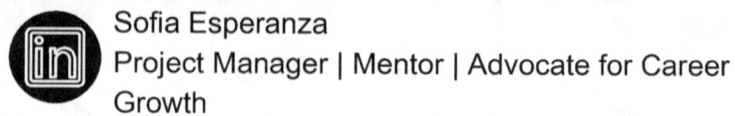

Sofia Esperanza
Project Manager | Mentor | Advocate for Career Growth

Hey Jeremy! ☺ I just wanted to drop you a quick message to share some tips as you embark on your journey as a Financial Analyst:

1. Network Relentlessly: Connect with your colleagues and other professionals in the industry. Attend networking events and don't hesitate to reach out for informational interviews.
2. Invest in Continuous Learning: Finance is always evolving. Consider enrolling in workshops, webinars, or online courses to stay updated on the latest trends and skills.
3. Build Your Credibility: Share your insights and knowledge on LinkedIn. Engaging with relevant content can help you establish your presence in the finance community.
4. Seek Mentorship: Look for a mentor who can guide you through your career journey. Having someone with experience can make a huge difference.

You're going to do great things, and I'm here to support you along the way! Let me know if you ever want to talk or need anything.

Prepare for Your New Role: If you're entering a new job or career, take some time to research your industry. Familiarize yourself with common terminology, trends, and key players.

Reach Out to Your Network: Don't hesitate to connect with colleagues or professionals in your desired field. Send a quick message or email introducing yourself and expressing your enthusiasm for networking.

Set Learning Goals: Identify areas where you'd like to grow professionally. Consider taking an online course or attending a workshop to enhance your skills.

Find a Mentor: Reflect on who in your network might be a good mentor. Reach out and ask if they'd be willing to share their insights and advice as you navigate your career.

Engage on Social Media: Start sharing your thoughts and experiences on platforms like LinkedIn. Engaging with others can help you build your professional presence and connect with like-minded individuals.

Remember, every successful professional started somewhere. Embrace the journey, keep learning, and trust in your abilities!

Chapter 3:
Kristina the Car
Mechanic

Querido Diario,

Kristina is one of the most inspiring people I've had the privilege to mentor. Her decision to enter the auto mechanic industry—a field dominated by men—shows a boldness that I deeply admire. It's not easy to challenge societal norms, but she does it with such passion and determination.

It makes me reflect on how important it is to pursue what truly drives us, even when the path isn't easy. Following our passion doesn't always align with what's expected of us, but that's where real growth and fulfillment happen. Kristina's journey reminds me that sometimes the most powerful thing we can do is embrace who we are, no matter what others might think.

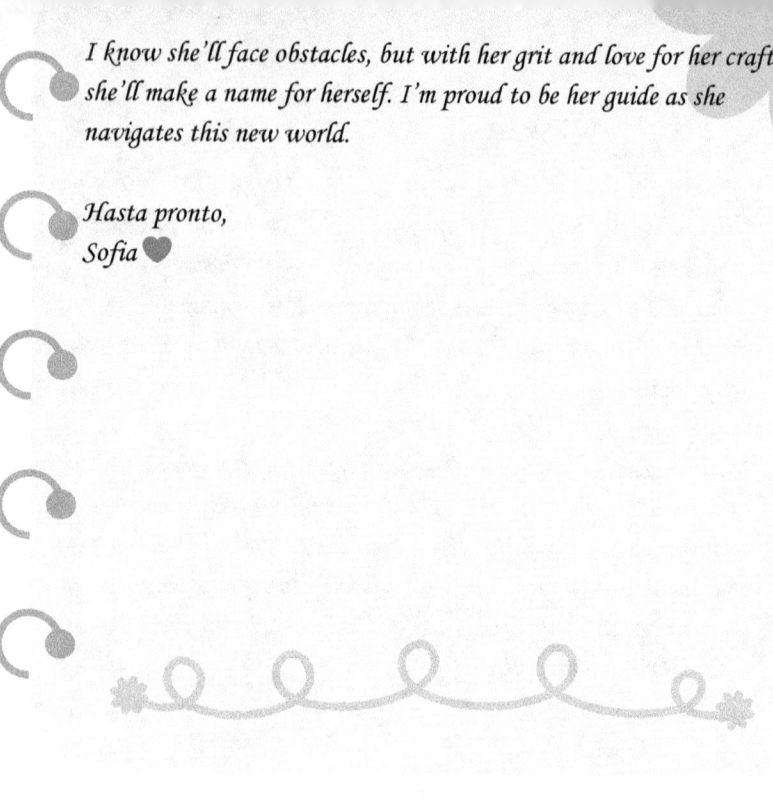

I know she'll face obstacles, but with her grit and love for her craft, she'll make a name for herself. I'm proud to be her guide as she navigates this new world.

Hasta pronto,
Sofia 🖤

Kristina

Hey Sofia, I started my first day at the shop today! It was kind of rough though. I feel like some of the guys there don't take me seriously because I'm a woman. 😕

Hey Kristina! I'm sorry to hear that. 😟 I know it's tough, but don't let anyone's attitude get to you. You're there because you've earned your place, and your skills will speak for themselves. Remember, breaking barriers isn't easy, but that's what makes you a trailblazer!

Yeah, I know you're right. It's just frustrating. Sometimes I feel like I have to work twice as hard to prove myself.

I get it. And you're absolutely right—it may feel that way sometimes. But here's the thing: your work ethic and dedication are going to set you apart. Stay confident, be persistent, and keep honing your skills.

Thanks, Sofia. I needed to hear that today. I'm not going to let them get in my head. I'm going to prove that I belong here!

That's the spirit! 🌟 Keep being you. And don't forget, building your personal brand as a mechanic is just as important. Make sure people know you're a pro and that you stand by your work. You've got this!

hansolo   ella.vator   maesharona   catmlem

 Kristina   ...

Kristina 📷 First day at the shop! Breaking barriers, one wrench at a time. 🔧 It's tough being underestimated, but I'm here to show that women belong in every field, including auto mechanics. 👊 #WomenInTrades #BreakingBarriers #FirstDayVibes #MechanicLife

Sofia You're amazing, Kristina! Keep showing up, putting in the work, and proving the doubters wrong. The best way to gain respect is through your consistency, professionalism, and passion. So proud of you for following your path! 💪🔧

Embrace Your Uniqueness: If you're working in a field where you're the minority, whether by gender, background, or experience, don't let that hold you back. Your perspective is valuable, and your passion is your power.

Build Your Personal Brand: Whether you're in the trades, corporate world, or any industry, make sure people know what you stand for. Share your expertise, experiences, and success stories on social media or professional networks like LinkedIn.

Stay Persistent: When facing challenges or feeling underestimated, remember that perseverance is key. Trust in your abilities and keep showing up, even when the going gets tough.

Seek Support: Find mentors or like-minded individuals who can provide encouragement and guidance, especially in difficult moments. Having a support system can help you stay grounded and focused.

Lead with Confidence: Confidence doesn't mean you won't have doubts—it means pushing forward despite them. Believe in the skills you've developed and lead with that self-assurance in every interaction.

Remember, your journey is unique, and there's power in forging your own path. No matter the obstacles, stay true to your passion and let your work speak for itself.

Chapter 4: Balancing Life and Career

Querido Diaro,

When I first started my career, I thought the only way to succeed was to put my head down and work as hard as possible, all the time. But as the years passed, I realized that burning the candle at both ends wasn't sustainable. I was exhausted, and my personal life was practically non-existent.

It wasn't until I had a conversation with Jamie that things shifted. She helped me understand that in order to thrive, not just survive, I needed to find balance. That meant setting boundaries, taking care of myself, and not feeling guilty about stepping away from work to recharge.

Now, as I mentor Jeremy and Kristina, I see that same pressure building up in them. They're just starting out, and there's a lot of excitement, but I know how easily that can turn into stress if they don't take the time to prioritize themselves.

Work-life balance isn't a luxury—it's a necessity. I just hope I can help them learn that sooner rather than later.

Hasta pronto,
Sofia 💜

Hey guys! I've been thinking a lot about work-life balance lately, and I wanted to share a few tips with you both. It's easy to get caught up in work, especially when you're just starting out. But trust me, finding time for yourself is so important. How's it going for you two?

Jeremy

Honestly, I'm still figuring it out. 😅 The hours are long, and sometimes I feel guilty when I take time off. Like I should be doing more.

Kristina

Same here. 😓 I love what I'm doing, but by the end of the week, I'm exhausted. It's hard to find time for anything else.

I've been there. It's really important to set boundaries early on. Take breaks during the day, and don't be afraid to log off or leave the garage on time. You'll actually be more productive when you're well-rested.

Jeremy

That makes sense. I've been trying to make time for the gym, but I always end up skipping it when work gets crazy.

Kristina

I've started going for walks in the morning to clear my head before the day starts. It helps a bit, but I still feel like I need more downtime.

Those are great steps! Keep it up, but also find hobbies that are just for fun. It's so easy to make everything about work, but we all need space to unwind and recharge. Trust me, taking care of yourselves now will set you up for long-term success.

Jeremy

You're right. I'll try to make time for that. Thanks, Sofia!

Kristina

Yeah, me too. Thanks for always looking out for us! 😊

Jamie - 1st
Career Coach | Author | Mentor | Speaker | Empowering Others to Achieve Their Full Potential

Hey Sofia, just checking in. How's everything going with mentoring Jeremy and Kristina? I know it can be a challenge to help others find balance, especially when they're so eager to make their mark.

Sofia

Hi Jamie! Things are going well. They're both working hard, but I can see the early signs of burnout. I've been encouraging them to set boundaries and find time for themselves, but it's definitely a work in progress.

Jamie

That's great advice. One thing I've found helpful with new professionals is reminding them that rest is part of productivity. A balanced life leads to better work in the long run. If they need resources, I've got a few books and articles I can send your way.

Sofia

That would be amazing! I'll definitely pass those along. Thanks for checking in, Jamie—I really appreciate it.

Jamie

Anytime! You're doing an awesome job guiding them through this phase. Keep up the good work!

Set Clear Boundaries: Whether you're starting a new job or navigating a busy career, it's crucial to set boundaries early on. Establish work hours, take breaks, and don't be afraid to say no when necessary.

Prioritize Self-Care: Self-care isn't just about spa days or vacations. It's about finding small ways to recharge each day— whether that's a morning walk, meditation, reading, or spending time with loved ones. Make time for the things that bring you joy.

Find Hobbies Outside of Work: Engaging in activities that have nothing to do with your job helps reduce stress and maintain balance. Whether it's exercising, cooking, painting, or volunteering, having a creative outlet will keep you energized.

Avoid Burnout: Recognize the signs of burnout—feeling overwhelmed, exhausted, or disconnected—and take action before it escalates. Regularly check in with yourself and make adjustments to your schedule if you're feeling drained.

Communicate Your Needs: Don't be afraid to talk to your boss or coworkers if you need to adjust your workload or schedule. Open communication can lead to better work-life balance and reduce unnecessary stress.

Remember, Rest is Productive: Taking time to rest isn't being lazy—it's being smart. You'll be more creative, focused, and productive if you allow yourself to recharge regularly.

Work-life balance takes practice and patience, but it's an essential part of long-term success. Start implementing these steps today to build a healthier and more fulfilling career.

Chapter 5: Navigating Challenges

Querido Diaro,

When I look back on the start of my career, I remember how many obstacles I faced. It wasn't smooth sailing at all. There were moments when I felt like giving up—whether it was being overlooked for a promotion, dealing with difficult coworkers, or not meeting my own expectations. But those tough times are what shaped me.

I learned that resilience isn't about never failing; it's about getting back up every time you do. Adaptability was also key. Things didn't always go the way I had planned, and I had to adjust, sometimes in ways I never anticipated.

If I could go back, I'd tell my younger self that challenges aren't roadblocks—they're stepping stones. Every obstacle I overcame made me stronger, more confident, and more prepared for what was to come. I want to make sure Jeremy and Kristina learn this lesson too, early on.

Hasta pronto,
Sofia ♥

Jeremy

Sofia, I could really use some advice. I just had a rough day at work. My manager didn't like the analysis I submitted, and it felt like all my hard work went unnoticed. It's so frustrating. Have you ever dealt with something like this?

Oh, Jeremy, I've been there more times than I can count! It's tough, especially when you've put so much effort into something. But setbacks are a normal part of the journey. What matters is how you respond.

It feels like a failure, though. I keep thinking, what if I'm just not cut out for this?

I know it feels that way, but trust me, this isn't a reflection of your abilities. It's an opportunity to learn. Think of it as feedback, not failure. I remember when I was in a similar position early in my career. I had to redo an entire project because my manager didn't like my approach. At first, I felt discouraged, but I used that experience to improve my skills and communication. It ended up being one of the best learning moments for me.

I didn't think of it like that. I guess I need to change my perspective and see what I can learn from this.

Exactly! Take a deep breath, look at the feedback objectively, and figure out how to apply it moving forward. The road to success is full of twists and turns, but you've got what it takes to make it through.

Thanks, Sofia. That really helped. I'm going to focus on what I can do better next time.

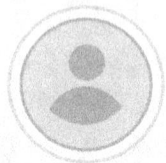   

hansolo   ella.vator   maesharona   catmlem

 Kristina   ...

Kristina 🔧 Tough day in the shop. Felt like no one took me seriously today, even though I was doing my best. Sometimes, it's hard being a woman in a male-dominated industry. ❄ #MechanicLife #BreakingBarriers

Sofia You're amazing, Kristina! Keep showing up, putting in the work, and proving the doubters wrong. The best way to gain respect is through your consistency, professionalism, and passion. So proud of you for following your path! 👏🙌

Embrace Challenges as Learning Opportunities: When you face a setback, ask yourself what you can learn from it. Feedback, even when it's hard to hear, is a tool for growth. Use it to refine your skills and approach.

Develop Resilience: Success doesn't come from never failing— it comes from how you bounce back after failure. The more resilient you are, the quicker you can recover and move forward.

Be Adaptable: The path to your career goals may not be linear. Be open to changing your approach when things don't go as planned. Flexibility is key to long-term success.

Don't Take Setbacks Personally: Remember that setbacks are not a reflection of your abilities or potential. It's easy to internalize criticism, but learning to separate feedback from your self-worth is crucial.

Assert Yourself: In situations where you feel disrespected, don't shy away from standing up for yourself. Assertiveness doesn't mean being aggressive—it means confidently expressing your value and boundaries.

Seek Support: Whether it's a mentor, friend, or coworker, find someone you can talk to when things get tough. Sometimes an outside perspective can provide the encouragement and advice you need to get back on track.

Challenges are a natural part of any career. How you navigate them will define your path. By viewing obstacles as opportunities and staying adaptable, you'll build the resilience needed for long-term success.

Chapter 6: Celebrating Success

Querido Diaro,

It's incredible how far we've all come. Watching Jeremy and Kristina evolve in their careers has been nothing short of inspiring. Jeremy is finding his footing as a Financial Analyst, building his network and credibility in the field. Kristina, on the other hand, is breaking down barriers in the auto industry and showing everyone what she's capable of.

I'm also proud of my own growth. Being a mentor has taught me more than I could have imagined. It's not just about giving advice—it's about listening, learning from their experiences, and seeing the potential in someone even before they see it in themselves. Jeremy and Kristina aren't the only ones growing; I've become stronger and more confident in my ability to guide others.

There's a deep satisfaction that comes from seeing someone you've mentored succeed, knowing you had a small part in their journey. But more than that, I'm proud of them for taking the leap, facing their fears, and achieving their goals. This is only the beginning for all of us.

Hasta pronto,
Sofia 🖤

Sofiia's LinkedIn Post

 Sofia Esperanza
Project Manager | Mentor | Advocate for Career
Growth

I'm so proud of my mentees, Jeremy and Kristina! Watching them grow and achieve their goals has been one of the most rewarding experiences in my career. Mentoring has not only given me the opportunity to guide them but has also helped me grow as a leader. There's something special about seeing others succeed and knowing you played a role in that process. Here's to many more successes! #Mentorship #Leadership #Growth

Jeremy
Financial Analyst | Data Enthusiast | Driven to Solve
Complex Problems

Excited to share that I've completed my first quarter as a
Financial Analyst! It's been a challenging but rewarding
journey, and I'm proud of how far I've come. Grateful for my
mentor Sofia and the support I've received from colleagues
along the way. Onward and upward! #FinancialAnalyst
#CareerGrowth #Milestones

Sofia Esperanza - 1st
Project Manager | Mentor | Advocate for Career Growth

So proud of how far you've come, Jeremy! This is only the
beginning for you. Keep pushing forward and striving for excellence.
🚀

Kristina

Automotive Technician | Breaking Barriers | Driven by Passion for Cars

Proud to say I've made it through my first few months as a mechanic! It hasn't always been easy, but I'm breaking barriers and proving that women belong in the trades. Special shoutout to Sofia for encouraging me to stay confident and true to myself. This is just the beginning! #WomenInTrades #BreakingBarriers #MechanicLife

Sofia Esperanza - 1st
Project Manager | Mentor | Advocate for Career Growth

You're breaking barriers every day, Kristina! Your determination and passion are inspiring. Keep up the amazing work.

I just saw both of your LinkedIn posts and I have to say, I'm bursting with pride. You've both accomplished so much in such a short time!

Kristina

Thanks, Sofia! It feels good to look back and see how far I've come, especially knowing how many times I felt like giving up.

Jeremy

Same here! I'm still learning every day, but it's nice to take a moment to celebrate the wins. I wouldn't be here without your guidance.

You've both done the hard work, and that's what matters. Don't forget to celebrate these milestones—it's important to recognize how far you've come. And remember, this is just the start of your journey. There's so much more to achieve!

Kristina

I'll toast to that!

Jeremy

Agreed! Here's to more growth and success in the future.

Let's keep supporting each other and pushing forward. I'm excited to see what's next for you both!

Celebrate Your Wins: Take time to acknowledge your achievements, no matter how big or small. Celebrating success is a way to build confidence and motivate yourself for the future.

Reflect on Your Growth: Look back at where you started and recognize the progress you've made. Reflection helps you understand the journey you've been on and prepares you for future challenges.

Acknowledge Your Mentors: Whether you're a mentor or a mentee, recognize the value of guidance and support in your career. If someone has helped you along the way, reach out and express your gratitude.

Set New Goals: After celebrating your achievements, think about what's next. Use your success as a springboard to set new, even bigger goals. Growth is an ongoing process.

Support Others on Their Journey: Pay it forward. If you've had a mentor, consider becoming one yourself. Helping others succeed can be just as fulfilling as your own success.

Stay Connected: Build relationships with people who support and challenge you. Surround yourself with a network that celebrates your successes and helps you grow.

Success is not just about reaching the finish line; it's about recognizing the progress you've made and using it to fuel your future goals. By celebrating your wins and reflecting on your journey, you'll be ready for whatever comes next.

Conclusion: The Journey Continues

Querido Diario,

As I sit here reflecting on the journey I've shared with Jeremy and Kristina, I can't help but feel a deep sense of fulfillment. When I first started mentoring them, I wasn't sure what to expect. I had my own doubts and worries, wondering if I could really make an impact. But looking at how far they've come—Jeremy finding his voice in the financial world, Kristina breaking barriers in the automotive industry —I'm reminded that growth happens in small, steady steps.

It's been a privilege to walk alongside them in this season of their lives, and I know this is just the beginning. They're going to do incredible things, and I'll be here to cheer them on every step of the way. I've learned so much from them too. Mentorship is a two-way street, and I'm grateful for the lessons they've taught me about resilience, passion, and the courage to pursue your dreams.

As for me, I look forward to continuing this journey—not just as a mentor but as someone always open to growth. There are new opportunities on the horizon, new people to inspire, and more lessons to learn. This journey doesn't end; it evolves.

Hasta pronto,
Sofia ♥

Sofia Esperanza
Project Manager | Mentor | Advocate for Career Growth

As my mentoring journey with Jeremy and Kristina comes to a significant milestone, I've been reflecting on the importance of giving back. Being a mentor has shown me that success isn't just about achieving your own goals—it's about lifting others up along the way.

To all the recent graduates and those early in their careers: Don't be afraid to reach out for guidance. Surround yourself with people who challenge you, who inspire you to grow. And when the time comes, pay it forward. Mentorship is one of the greatest gifts you can give—and receive.

Here are a few final tips I've learned along the way:

1. Stay curious. Never stop learning, whether you're just starting out or well into your career.
2. Build a strong network. Relationships matter. Invest time in creating meaningful connections.
3. Embrace failure. Every setback is an opportunity to grow. Learn from it and move forward.
4. Follow your passion. Success comes when you pursue what truly drives you. Don't settle for anything less.

Mentoring has enriched my life in ways I never expected, and I encourage everyone to find ways to give back. The journey is never truly over—it's always evolving.
#Mentorship #CareerTips #Leadership #Growth

Jamie:

Hey Sofia, I've been following your journey with Jeremy and Kristina, and I have to say, you've done a phenomenal job. Watching them grow under your mentorship has been inspiring.

Thank you, Jamie! It's been a rewarding experience. I've learned so much along the way.

That's what mentorship is all about. You've not only helped them succeed but also grown as a leader yourself. Keep going, Sofia. Your impact goes beyond just the two of them—your story will inspire many more to take that leap of faith.

I hope so. It's been an incredible journey, and I'm looking forward to what's next!

No doubt. You're just getting started. Keep inspiring others, and don't be afraid to take on more challenges. You've got this!

Reflect on Your Journey: Take a moment to think about how far you've come in your career. Reflection is key to understanding your progress and preparing for future growth.

Seek Mentorship: If you don't already have a mentor, consider reaching out to someone who can guide you. Whether you're just starting or looking to advance, mentorship is invaluable.

Be Open to Learning: Growth doesn't stop once you've achieved your initial goals. Stay open to new opportunities and continue learning—both in your field and in life.

Pay It Forward: When the time is right, become a mentor yourself. Sharing your knowledge and experiences with others is one of the most rewarding ways to give back.

Celebrate Your Growth: Recognize your accomplishments and the lessons learned along the way. It's important to celebrate how far you've come before moving on to the next challenge.

Stay Connected: Maintain your relationships with mentors, peers, and colleagues. Strong networks will continue to support you in your journey, and you'll have the opportunity to support others in theirs.

Success isn't just a destination—it's a journey. By reflecting on where you are, seeking guidance when needed, and paying it forward, you can continue to grow and inspire others. Your journey is just beginning!

Diary-Style Reflections

Networking:
One of the biggest lessons I've learned is that who you know can be just as important as what you know. Early in my career, I used to think networking was transactional, but I've since realized it's about building genuine relationships. Whether you're connecting with peers, mentors, or industry leaders, approach every relationship with authenticity. Don't be afraid to ask for advice, but also be willing to offer help when you can.

Practical Tip: Start attending industry events, whether in person or virtually. Don't be afraid to reach out to someone after an event and follow up with a personal note or message on LinkedIn. The key is to stay connected!

Building a Personal Brand:
Your personal brand is the impression you leave on others. It's how people see you, both online and in real life. Early on, I struggled with defining my brand. I thought it was just about being professional, but it's also about being authentic. For me, it's a mix of being driven, empathetic, and committed to personal growth. It's important that your brand reflects who you are and what you stand for.

Practical Tip: Make sure your LinkedIn profile aligns with your values, goals, and skills. Think about the story you want to tell. Every post, comment, or interaction should reflect that narrative.

Resilience is key in navigating any career. There will be moments when you doubt yourself or face setbacks, but it's how you bounce back that matters most. For me, it was in those moments of failure that I learned the most valuable lessons. Each challenge helped me grow stronger and better prepared for the next step.

Practical Tip: When facing a difficult situation, take a step back and reflect on what you can learn from it. Surround yourself with a supportive network and remember—it's okay to ask for help. Resilience isn't about doing everything on your own.

Work-Life Balance:

In my early years and even some later years, I thought success meant working non-stop, but I quickly learned that burnout isn't worth it. Balance is about making time for what truly matters—your health, family, hobbies, and rest. You'll be more effective at work when you're taking care of yourself outside of work too.

Practical Tip: Set boundaries. It's okay to say no to extra work if it compromises your well-being. Find hobbies that bring you joy and give your mind a break from the daily grind.

LinkedIn Post: Announcing Career Milestone

Here's a sample post you can adapt to share your achievements and goals:

✦ Exciting News! ✦

I'm thrilled to announce that I've officially [landed my first job/secured a promotion] as [Job Title] at [Company Name]! 🎉 It's been an incredible journey, and I'm grateful to everyone who supported me along the way. Special thanks to [mentor, colleague, or supporter] for their guidance.

As I step into this new chapter, I'm eager to continue learning, growing, and contributing to [industry/field]. Here's to the next adventure!

#CareerGoals #NewBeginnings #LearningAndGrowing

LinkedIn Message: Requesting a Mentorship Opportunity

Need to reach out to a potential mentor? Here's a template:

Hi [Name],

I hope this message finds you well. I've been following your work in [industry/field] for some time now, and I'm incredibly inspired by your career journey and insights.

I'm currently in the early stages of my career as a [Job Title] at [Company Name], and I'm eager to continue learning and growing in this space. I would be honored if you'd consider mentoring me. I'd love the opportunity to learn from your experiences and gain your advice on navigating the challenges and opportunities in this field.

Thank you so much for considering this request. I look forward to the possibility of connecting further.

Best regards,
[Your Name]

LinkedIn Post: Sharing a Personal Career Story

Here's a template to share a meaningful career moment:

When I first started in [industry], I didn't know what to expect. I had doubts, fears, and many challenges along the way. But through resilience, determination, and the support of mentors, I've grown both professionally and personally.

Today, I'm proud to share that I've reached a milestone in my journey as [Job Title] at [Company Name]. It hasn't always been easy, but I'm excited to keep pushing forward, learning, and making an impact.

To anyone just starting out: keep going. Every step forward counts. Don't hesitate to seek out mentors, take on challenges, and remember—you're not alone in this journey.

#CareerGrowth #Resilience #MentorshipMatters

Social Media Templates

LinkedIn Message: Networking Follow-Up

Following up with a connection after an event? Try this message:

Hi [Name],

It was a pleasure meeting you at [event/conference] last week! I really enjoyed our conversation about [topic discussed], and I would love to stay connected.

I'd be interested in hearing more about your work in [industry/role], and I'm always open to opportunities to collaborate or exchange ideas. Let's keep in touch!

Best regards,
[Your Name]

Use These Templates: Adapt the LinkedIn posts and messages to your own style and career goals. Personalize them to reflect your journey.

Build Your Personal Brand: Think about what you want to be known for and make sure your online presence aligns with that vision. Be authentic.

Start Networking: Take the leap and connect with professionals in your field. Don't hesitate to ask for advice or guidance.

Stay Resilient: Challenges will come, but each one is an opportunity to grow. Keep moving forward, and don't be afraid to ask for help when needed.

Prioritize Balance: As you start your career, remember to prioritize your health and well-being alongside your professional goals.

Further Reading

- **Books:**
  - Lean In: Women, Work, and the Will to Lead by Sheryl Sandberg
    - A powerful guide on leadership, balancing career and personal life, and pursuing professional growth.
  - What Color is Your Parachute? A Practical Manual for Job-Hunters and Career-Changers by Richard N. Bolles
    - This classic career guide offers tools for finding purpose in your career and navigating career transitions.
  - Grit: The Power of Passion and Perseverance by Angela Duckworth
    - A deep dive into how grit and determination can be more critical than talent when achieving long-term success.
  - Dare to Lead: Brave Work. Tough Conversations. Whole Hearts. by Brené Brown
    - A call to embrace vulnerability as a strength and a guide to becoming a courageous and empathetic leader.

- **Articles:**
  - "The Importance of Mentorship" by Harvard Business Review
    - This article discusses how to find and benefit from mentorship relationships throughout your career.
  - "How to Build Your Personal Brand" by Forbes
    - Practical tips on building a personal brand that stands out in today's competitive job market.
  - "The Science of Resilience" by The New York Times
    - An exploration of how resilience is developed and why it's key to personal and professional growth.

- LinkedIn Learning
  - Offers a wide variety of online courses focused on leadership, communication skills, and career development.
- Coursera
  - Provides courses from top universities and companies on topics like negotiation, business strategy, and career success.
- Glassdoor Blog
  - Career advice and insights into company culture to help you navigate your job search and grow in your career.

Born and raised in Spanish Harlem, Myriam has spent the last few years living in Florida with her husband and four dogs.

With over 30 years of experience in the Retirement Industry, she has honed her skills as a leader, mentor, and coach, guiding individuals both personally and professionally towards success and growth.

Despite being an introvert, Myriam has a unique ability to engage in meaningful conversations and uses her compelling speaking voice to advocate for her faith and her passion for helping others reach their full potential.

As the coordinator of Real Talk with Victor and co-owner of the nonprofit 1240 to 3:16 Ministries alongside her husband, Myriam is deeply committed to serving communities through prison ministry and local and global outreach initiatives. Her dedication to making a difference extends beyond the professional realm, as she actively participates in church activities and contributes to various community-driven endeavors.

Explore More in the
Now What? Series

Inspiration and guidance for every stage in life.

Now What? A Journey to Future Career Success

"An inspiring guide to navigating career transitions, setting goals, and unlocking your potential for success."

Available on Amazon

Stay tuned for more exciting titles coming soon!
Visit www.myriamcmuniz.com to join the journey.